STRATEGY FOR HOMELAND DEFENSE AND DEFENSE SUPPORT OF CIVIL AUTHORITIES

February 2013

DISTRIBUTION:
SECRETARIES OF THE MILITARY DEPARTMENTS
CHAIRMAN OF THE JOINT CHIEFS OF STAFF
UNDER SECRETARIES OF DEFENSE
DEPUTY CHIEF MANAGEMENT OFFICER
CHIEFS OF THE MILITARY SERVICES
COMMANDERS OF THE COMBATANT COMMANDS
CHIEF OF THE NATIONAL GUARD BUREAU
DIRECTOR, COST ASSESSMENT AND PROGRAM EVALUATION
DIRECTOR, OPERATIONAL TEST AND EVALUATION
GENERAL COUNSEL OF THE DEPARTMENT OF DEFENSE
INSPECTOR GENERAL OF THE DEPARTMENT OF DEFENSE
ASSISTANT SECRETARIES OF DEFENSE
DEPARTMENT OF DEFENSE CHIEF INFORMATION OFFICER
ASSISTANTS TO THE SECRETARY OF DEFENSE
DIRECTOR, ADMINISTRATION AND MANAGEMENT
DIRECTOR, NET ASSESSMENT
DIRECTORS OF THE DEFENSE AGENCIES
DIRECTORS OF THE DOD FIELD ACTIVITIES

SECRETARY OF DEFENSE
1000 DEFENSE PENTAGON
WASHINGTON, DC 20301-1000

FEB 2 5 2013

MEMORANDUM FOR: SEE DISTRIBUTION

SUBJECT: Strategy for Homeland Defense and Defense Support of Civil Authorities

The attached *Strategy for Homeland Defense and Defense Support of Civil Authorities* provides innovative guidance and charts a fiscally sustainable course for our homeland defense and civil support priorities and activities for the period 2012-2020. It ensures that the Department remains postured to deal with a range of potential threats, both conventional and asymmetric, and to provide support to civil authorities in the event that prevention fails. For the first time, the Strategy also addresses the Department's response to those most dire events – complex catastrophes – that have the capability to overwhelm civil authorities and cause severe, cascading effects.

I expect that all DoD Components will incorporate the tenets and direction of this Strategy into their foundational documents, guidance, concepts of operations, and activities.

The Assistant Secretary of Defense for Homeland Defense and Americas' Security Affairs will be responsible for ensuring implementation and institutionalization of this Strategy and will report to me periodically on implementation progress.

Attachment:
As stated

FOREWORD

I am releasing this new *Strategy for Homeland Defense and Defense Support of Civil Authorities* to elaborate priorities for these core Department of Defense (DoD) missions. This Strategy reflects the direction of the Department's civilian and military leadership and the advice of our Federal preparedness partners. It postures DoD to address the range of current and emerging threats to the homeland and natural and manmade hazards inside the United States for the period 2012-2020, and it is in keeping with current fiscal realities.

This Strategy relies first and foremost on those partnerships that are vital to DoD's ability to successfully fulfill its homeland defense and civil support missions. These partnerships occur on multiple levels and include other Federal departments and agencies; State, local, Tribal, and Territorial authorities; private sector owners of defense-related industries and critical infrastructure; and our international partners.

This Strategy also highlights the Department's priority efforts to expand unity of effort with State and local first responders; achieve an integrated planning approach with Federal and State authorities; ensure the continuous performance of DoD's mission essential functions in an all-hazards environment; protect and improve the resilience of the Force; and bridge gaps in preparedness for catastrophic events.

The American people are served by the world's finest military. This Strategy ensures that as threats to the homeland evolve over the next decade the men and women of DoD will be prepared to defend our Nation and support our people in their time of need.

Leon E. Panetta

TABLE OF CONTENTS

EXECUTIVE SUMMARY

We are now moving beyond traditional distinctions between homeland and national security. National security draws on the strength and resilience of our citizens, communities, and economy. This includes a determination to prevent terrorist attacks against the American people by fully coordinating the actions that we take abroad with the actions and precautions that we take at home. It must also include a commitment to building a more secure and resilient nation, while maintaining open flows of goods and people. We will continue to develop the capacity to address the threats and hazards that confront us, while redeveloping our infrastructure to secure our people and work cooperatively with other nations.

National Security Strategy
May 2010

Defending U.S. territory and the people of the United States is the highest priority of the Department of Defense (DoD), and providing appropriate defense support of civil authorities (DSCA) is one of the Department's primary missions.[1] This *Strategy for Homeland Defense and Defense Support of Civil Authorities* orients the Department towards an increasingly complex strategic environment. It emphasizes innovative approaches, greater integration, deepening of external partnerships, and increased effectiveness and efficiencies in DoD's homeland activities. It applies the vital capabilities of the Total Force – in the Active and Reserve Components – to make the nation more secure and resilient. Finally, the Strategy guides future decisions on homeland defense and civil support issues consistent with the *Defense Strategic Guidance* and the *Quadrennial Defense Review (QDR)*.

This Strategy identifies two priority missions for the Department's activities in the homeland from 2012 to 2020. DoD works with the Department of Homeland Security (DHS) and other actors to achieve these missions:

- Defend U.S. territory from direct attack by state and non-state actors; and

- Provide assistance to domestic civil authorities in the event of natural or manmade disasters, potentially in response to a very significant or catastrophic event.

These priority missions are reinforced, supported, or otherwise enabled through the pursuit of the following objectives:

- Counter air and maritime threats at a safe distance;

- Prevent terrorist attacks on the homeland through support to law enforcement;

- Maintain preparedness for domestic Chemical, Biological, Radiological, Nuclear (CBRN) incidents; and

- Develop plans and procedures to ensure Defense Support of Civil Authorities during complex catastrophes.

---

[1] As defined by "Sustaining U.S. Global Leadership: Priorities for the 21st Century Defense," January 2012.

This Strategy also defines a number of other priority lines of effort, or *strategic approaches*, that are intended to enhance the effectiveness of the Department's homeland defense and civil support efforts. Although these items require a distinct departmental effort, they do so without adding significant resource requirements. These are:

- Assure DoD's ability to conduct critical missions;

- Promote Federal-State unity of effort;

- Conduct integrated planning with Federal and State authorities; and

- Expand North American cooperation to strengthen civil support.

Defending the homeland neither begins nor ends at U.S. borders, and departmental planning is guided by the concept of an active, layered defense – a *global* defense that aims to deter and defeat aggression abroad and simultaneously protect the homeland. It is a defense-in-depth that relies on collection, analysis, and sharing of information and intelligence; strategic and regional deterrence; military presence in forward regions; and the ability to rapidly generate and project warfighting capabilities to defend the United States, its Allies, and its interests.

The homeland is a functioning theater of operations, where DoD regularly performs a wide range of defense and civil support activities through U.S. Northern Command (in concert with the North American Aerospace Defense Command, or NORAD), U.S. Pacific Command, and other DoD components. When faced with a crisis in the homeland – for example, a complex catastrophe as a result of an attack against the Nation or a natural disaster – DoD must be prepared to respond rapidly to this crisis while sustaining other defense and civil support operations. Within the homeland, arriving late to need is not an option.

The Department acts globally to defend the United States and its interests in all domains – land, air, maritime, space, and cyberspace – and similarly must be prepared to defend the homeland and support civil authorities in all domains. This Strategy is nested within a series of mutually supporting defense strategies and national guidance that provide policy and direction for the space and cyberspace domains, including the *National Security Space Strategy*, the *Ballistic Missile Defense Review*, and the *Defense Strategy for Operating in Cyberspace*. Other related and supporting strategies include the *DoD Mission Assurance Strategy*, *Presidential Policy Directive 8 – National Preparedness*, and *Homeland Security Presidential Directive 25 – Arctic Region Policy*. Finally, an active, layered defense of the homeland cannot be accomplished unilaterally nor conducted exclusively with military capabilities. The *Western Hemisphere Defense Policy*, the *Strategy to Combat Transnational Organized Crime*, the *National Strategy for Counterterrorism*, the *National Strategy for Global Supply Chain Security* and other regional and functional strategies articulate a range of defense, diplomatic, law enforcement, and capacity-building activities that the United States pursues with its neighbors to build an integrated, mutually-supportive concept of security.

The Department must weigh the objectives of this Strategy against the other priority areas described in the 2012 *Defense Strategic Guidance* and 2010 *QDR*. The defense of the homeland remains an important part of our decision calculus as we size and shape the future Joint Force. U.S. forces must be capable of deterring and defeating aggression by an opportunistic adversary in one region even when our forces are committed to a large-scale operation elsewhere. DoD must also consider the homeland defense mission while ensuring it can still confront more than one aggressor, anywhere in the world. Additionally, when the Department must make resource or force structure tradeoffs between homeland defense and civil support missions, it is DoD policy to first prioritize the fulfillment of the Department's responsibilities for homeland defense. As a second priority, this Strategy seeks to ensure that DoD is able to support civil authorities during catastrophic events, including a complex catastrophe, within the homeland.

I. STRATEGIC CONTEXT

The rapid proliferation of destructive technologies, combined with potent ideologies of violent extremism, requires sustaining a high level of vigilance against terrorist threats. Moreover, state adversaries are acquiring new means to strike targets at greater distances from their borders and with greater lethality. The United States must also be prepared to respond to the full range of potential natural disasters.

Quadrennial Defense Review Report
February 2010

This *Strategy for Homeland Defense and Defense Support of Civil Authorities* is the result of a dynamic set of variables. National security threats, hazards, vulnerabilities, strategic guidance, and political and economic factors have evolved since the first *Strategy for Homeland Defense and Civil Support* was issued in 2005, and the Department must posture the Total Force to address these new realities. This Strategy flows from national-level security and defense guidance documents and amplifies their direction related to defense of the homeland and civil support.

Figure 2: Standing guidance

The 2010 National Security Strategy *states that "the Administration has no greater responsibility than the safety and security of the American people." It gives particular focus to strengthening public-private partnerships to maintain vital operations if disaster strikes the nation's critical infrastructure – most of which is held by the private sector – and to improving resilience. It also emphasizes improved and expanded information and intelligence sharing among Federal agencies and with State and local partners to prevent attacks in the homeland.*

The 2011 National Strategy for Counterterrorism *gives primacy to whole-of-government efforts to counter terrorism, highlights the danger of terrorist pursuit of weapons of mass destruction (WMD), and directs the continuation of investments in aviation, maritime, and border-security capabilities and information sharing to make the United States a hardened and increasingly difficult target for terrorists to penetrate.*

Presidential Policy Directive-8 National Preparedness (PPD-8) *aims to strengthen the security and resilience of the United States through systematic preparation for the threats that pose the greatest risk to the security of the Nation, including acts of terrorism, cyber attacks, pandemics, and catastrophic natural disasters. It establishes a National Preparedness Goal and a National Preparedness System of interagency frameworks and plans to prevent, protect against, respond to, recover from, and mitigate the effects of those threats that pose the greatest risk to the Nation. DoD shares responsibility for national preparedness efforts and is required to support interagency planning under PPD-8.*

The 2010 Quadrennial Defense Review *establishes defense of the United States and support of civil authorities at home as key missions of the Department. It directs enhancements to improve the readiness and flexibility of DoD's chemical, biological, radiological, and nuclear (CBRN) consequence management response forces in recognition of the proliferation of destructive technologies and the potent ideologies of violent extremism.*

Security environment: threats, hazards, and vulnerabilities

The security environment for the homeland is characterized by a variety of nation-state and terrorist threats, natural and manmade hazards, and a host of physical and network vulnerabilities.

Threats: Al-Qaeda is on the path to defeat, but its adherents continue to plan acts of violence in the United States. Additionally, loosely-networked individuals not affiliated with identified terror organizations, but inspired by the Al-Qaeda narrative, pose a continued threat. This includes homegrown violent extremists (HVEs), who may be inspired to conduct their own attacks; they are less dependent on operational support from overseas terrorist groups, but could be highly lethal. They are encouraged through chat rooms and social media, trained to produce complex improvised explosive devices (IEDs) through extremist websites, and facilitated by commonly available communications and information technology that enhance planning, target surveillance, operational security, and attack execution. Various plots – like the Times Square car bomber and attempts to attack transportation nodes in New York City and Washington, DC – exemplify this growing HVE threat.

U.S. military personnel and facilities are visible symbols of American power, and they will remain primary targets for HVEs, including "insider threats" within the Armed Forces, as seen at Fort Hood in 2009. The growing pattern of attempted and actual attacks on military personnel and facilities – such as recruiting centers, National Guard armories, Armed Forces Reserve Centers, and the Pentagon – pose a significant, growing, and enduring challenge to military force protection and anti-terrorism requirements.

Challenges remain in the detection, monitoring, and interdiction of threats in the air and maritime domains. Threats can appear in the form of small "go fast" boats and ultra-light aircraft, waterborne IEDs, hijacked commercial aircraft or ships, and semi- and fully-submersible vessels and other conveyances adapted for illicit activities. Similarly, illicit trafficking and transnational criminal organizations pose a continuous challenge to the security and integrity of all homeland domains, including U.S. land borders with Canada and Mexico and maritime borders in the Caribbean Sea and Pacific Ocean.

The proliferation of weapons of mass destruction (WMD) capabilities and means of delivery to adversary nation-states, combined with terrorists' interest in obtaining WMD, represent direct, high consequence, and serious physical threats to the homeland. Through WMD, state and non-state adversaries actively seek to inflict mass civilian casualties in the United States, cripple our economy, or disrupt U.S. military operations overseas.

Threats to our national cyber infrastructure from a range of state and non-state actors continue to be a deep concern for the Department. Terrorists and criminals increasingly exploit the Internet to communicate, organize, and conduct training and operational planning; hacker networks are demonstrating an increasing sophistication in their ability to target networks and exploit data; and hostile foreign governments have the technical and financial resources to support advanced network exploitation and launch attacks on the informational and physical elements of our cyber infrastructure.

Hazards: The 2011 Great Eastern Japan earthquake, tsunami, and nuclear reactor disaster created a complex catastrophe of immense scope. A similar convergence of a large-scale natural disaster and a resulting manmade crisis or technological failure could result in a complex catastrophe in the United States, with cascading effects that overwhelm national response and recovery capabilities.[2] In addition, the homeland will continue to experience manmade and natural hazards of varying types and severity that will test the response capabilities of Federal, State[3], local, Tribal, and Territorial authorities.

Vulnerabilities: Contemporary threats and hazards are magnified by the vulnerabilities created by the increasingly interconnected nature of information systems, critical infrastructure, and supply chains. The information networks and industrial control systems owned by DoD, and those maintained by commercial service providers and infrastructure operators, are subjected to increasingly sophisticated cyber intrusions and are vulnerable to physical attack and natural and manmade disasters. A targeted cyber or kinetic attack on the nation's commercial electrical infrastructure would not only degrade DoD mission essential functions but also impact DoD sustainment operations that depend on commercial electricity for fuel distribution, communications, and transportation. In the context of this increasingly interconnected security environment, seemingly isolated or remote incidents can cause substantial physical effects, degrade Defense systems, and quickly be transformed into significant or catastrophic events.[4]

Figure 3: Cyber threats

Working closely with the Department of Homeland Security, the Federal Bureau of Investigation, and other interagency partners, DoD plays a crucial role in supporting a national effort to confront cyber threats to critical infrastructure. DoD has developed the capability to conduct effective operations to counter threats to critical infrastructure and will take action to defend the Nation from cyber attack when directed by the President. Such operations will be done in a manner consistent with the policy principles and legal frameworks that DoD follows for other domains, including the law of armed conflict.

Increasing expectations

Public expectations for a decisive, fast, and effective Federal response to disasters have grown in the past decade, particularly in the wake of Hurricane Katrina. Although DoD is always in a support role to civilian authorities (primarily the Federal Emergency Management Agency, or FEMA) for disaster response, the capacity, capabilities, training, and professionalism of the Armed Forces mean that DoD is often expected to play a prominent supporting role in response efforts. The prevailing "go big, go early, go fast, be smart" approach to saving lives and protecting property in the homeland – evident during the preparations for and response to Hurricane Irene in August 2011 and particularly Hurricane Sandy in October 2012 – requires

---

[2] For example, planning scenarios indicate that a 7.7 magnitude earthquake along the New Madrid fault in the central United States could inflict ten times as many casualties as did Hurricane Katrina, across eight states, with cascading failures of "lifeline" critical infrastructure – including the power grid, water distribution, public health and transportation systems – with broad regional and national impact.

[3] Unless otherwise noted, "State" and/or "SLTT" refer collectively to State, local, Tribal, and Territorial entities throughout this document.

[4] The Defense Strategy for Operating in Cyberspace addresses the threats to and defense of the cyber domain. The *Strategy for Homeland Defense and Defense Support of Civil Authorities* is concerned with mitigating the physical effects of a cyber attack when requested by civil authorities, and ensuring the continuous performance of the Department's mission essential functions – many of which rely upon cyber connectivity.

DoD to rapidly and effectively harness resources to quickly respond to civil support requests in the homeland.

Fiscal realities

The balance between available resources and our security needs has never been more delicate.

Sustaining U.S. Global Leadership:
Priorities for 21st Century Defense
January 2012

This Strategy amplifies the homeland defense and civil support priorities elaborated in the *National Security Strategy, Report of the Quadrennial Defense Review, and Defense Strategic Guidance*. It is driven by the imperative to defend the United States, save lives, and protect property in an era of higher expectations. It is also informed by fiscal realities so that it may be fully implemented and sustainable in the period 2012-2020.

DoD budget austerity requires rigorous mission needs analysis and risk-based decision making in order to ensure Defense operations and activities in the homeland are adequately considered among priorities for capability development or preservation. In the current fiscal environment, DoD must adequately manage risk among its primary defense missions and associated capabilities. This Strategy therefore elaborates innovative approaches, articulates mission priorities, guides the deepening of external partnerships, and creatively adapts existing and programmed capabilities, rather than directing large investments in new equipment and capabilities. In so doing, it addresses the complex security environment and new operational paradigms for DoD's missions in the homeland in a responsible, sustainable manner.

Assumptions

This Strategy is built upon the following key assumptions:

- The likelihood of a conventional military attack on the U.S. homeland by a nation-state is very low.

- Threats to the homeland will significantly increase when the United States is engaged in contingency operations with an adversary abroad.

- Potential nation-state adversaries will continue to refine asymmetric attack plans against the homeland as part of their concepts of operation and broader military strategies of confrontation with the United States.

- State, non-state, and criminal cyber attacks on DoD networks will grow in number, intensity, and complexity, as will attacks on public-private information systems and critical infrastructure networks on which DoD depends.

- Terrorists will continue to pursue attacks inside the homeland, including use of WMD to inflict mass casualties.

- Loosely-networked or individually motivated violent extremists will continue to exhort followers and encourage violent extremism in the homeland.

    o HVEs will operate alone or organize in small groups and will be largely autonomous in their operations; they will have access to web-based resources to assist them in their operational planning.

    o Military members and facilities will remain prominent targets of terrorists, and particularly by HVEs.

- DoD will be called upon to provide significant resources and capabilities during a catastrophic event in the homeland.

    o The National Response Framework will remain the primary instrument for applying Federal capabilities during disaster response.

II. MISSIONS, OBJECTIVES, AND CORE CAPABILITIES

This Strategy – together with other national security and defense strategies – leads to an end state in which the homeland remains secure from direct attack and the Total Force can ably support domestic civil authorities in conjunction with Federal, State, and local authorities and the private sector. This Strategy defines objectives and describes the core capabilities needed to meet these objectives, as summarized in Figure 4.

Missions	Objectives	Core Capabilities
1) Defend U.S. Territory From Direct Attack by State and Non-State Actors	*a. Counter air and maritime threats at a safe distance*	• Persistent air & maritime domain awareness • Capable, responsive air defense forces • Capable, responsive maritime forces
	b. Prevent terrorist attacks on the homeland through support to law enforcement	• Rapid and actionable intelligence on terrorist threats • Capabilities to counter IEDs • Capabilities to prevent terrorists' use of WMD in the homeland • Rapid acquisition, analysis, and dissemination of threat information • Programs to counter insider threats • Dual-effect military training
2) Provide Defense Support of Civil Authorities (DSCA)	*a. Maintain Defense preparedness for domestic CBRN*	• Postured, rapidly deployable CBRN response forces
	b. Develop plans and procedures to ensure DSCA during complex catastrophes.	• Immediate response authority • Geographically-proximate force sourcing • Ready access to non-National Guard Reserve forces

Figure 4: Missions, Objectives and Core Capabilities

Mission 1: Defend U.S. Territory from Direct Attack by State and Non-State Actors

Due to the wide array of potential attack vectors, DoD embraces a homeland defense concept that relies first upon an active, layered global defense, and in the event that defense fails, a series of overlapping capabilities to detect, deter, deny, and defeat threats. This Strategy provides guidance for more effective performance of this core mission and elaborates priorities for the Department's homeland defense activities.[5]

Objective 1.a: Counter air and maritime threats at a safe distance

DoD has primary responsibility for protecting the United States from *air threats* – including manned aircraft, unmanned aircraft, and cruise missiles – whether in the approaches or within

---

[5] The 2010 *Ballistic Missile Defense Review* summarizes the U.S. defense strategy for protecting the homeland from limited ballistic missile attack. The 2011 *National Security Space Strategy* charts a path for leveraging emerging opportunities to strengthen U.S. national security space posture. The 2011 *Defense Strategy for Operating in Cyberspace* guides the Department towards a comprehensive cyberspace posture.

U.S. airspace. This responsibility is carried out in partnership with Canada, through NORAD. While DoD has sole responsibility for *defeating* air threats, it receives assistance from the Federal Aviation Administration (FAA) and DHS assets for early identification of anomalous air activity which may ultimately threaten the United States.

To counter and defeat *maritime threats* at a safe distance, DoD partners with DHS and optimizes the mutually supporting capabilities and relationships between the Navy and the Coast Guard.[6] DoD maintains alert Navy ships and aircraft for homeland defense operations and has standing procedures to provide U.S. Northern Command (USNORTHCOM), U.S. Pacific Command (USPACOM), and NORAD with additional forces when necessary to conduct homeland defense missions in territorial waters or in the maritime approaches to the United States.

DoD will prioritize the continued enhancement of three critical capabilities in the period to 2020 to counter maritime and air threats at a safe distance from U.S. territory and the approaches:

- Persistent air and maritime domain awareness;

- Capable and responsive air defense forces; and

- Capable and responsive maritime forces.

<u>Persistent air and maritime domain awareness</u>[7]

DoD will work closely with Federal, private sector, and international partners to continually improve awareness of the air and maritime domains.

The U.S. Government (USG) faces major challenges in its ability to detect, identify, track, and if necessary, respond to threats in the air and maritime domains, given the daily volume of vessels, aircraft, and cargoes approaching, entering and departing North American ports of entry. Consistent with the 2010 *QDR* and the National Plans for Maritime and Air Domain Awareness, DoD works with interagency partners to enhance capabilities for domain awareness to monitor the air and maritime domains comprehensively for potential threats to the United States.

The *air domain* presents both challenges and partnership opportunities. DoD has expanded domain awareness since 9/11 by coordinating with interagency partners, improving radar surveillance, and expanding information sharing. DoD will emphasize collaboration with the

---

[6] As stated in the *2007 Cooperative Strategy for 21st Century Seapower*, "[m]aritime forces will defend the homeland by identifying and neutralizing threats as far from our shores as possible...our homeland defense effort will integrate across the maritime services, the Joint Force, the interagency community, our international partners and the private sector to provide the highest level of security possible."

[7] The 2005 *National Plan to Achieve Maritime Domain Awareness* defines "persistent awareness" as the integrated management of a diverse set of collection and processing capabilities, operated to detect and understand the activity of interest with sufficient sensor dwell, revisit rate, and required quality to expeditiously assess adversary actions, predict adversary plans, deny sanctuary to an adversary, and assess results of U.S./coalition actions. In terms of resources, "persistent" refers to an ability to maintain awareness anywhere on the globe. It is not meant to imply that DoD or the USG can or should simultaneously maintain awareness over the entire globe.

FAA and DHS to ensure that military air defense and security capabilities are integrated into the Next Generation (NEXTGEN) Air Traffic Control System. Such collaboration is also needed to reduce the number of unintentional civilian intrusions into restricted airspace.

The *maritime domain* is multi-jurisdictional, with various U.S. agencies responsible for tracking maritime traffic, including vessels, cargo, and people, from port of origin to arrival in the United States – a situation that creates many potential vulnerabilities. DoD – in partnership with DHS, the Department of Transportation (DoT), the Intelligence Community (IC), and private maritime companies – will reduce these vulnerabilities through the interconnected use of shore-, air-, space-, and sea-based radars and sensors, and information systems. By persistently monitoring the maritime domain, DoD and its partners will identify potential maritime threats in a timely manner and enhance operational decision making.

Capable and responsive air defense forces

DoD will regularly assess, size, and posture the forces assigned to protect and defend U.S. air sovereignty based upon the air threat, available resources, and national priorities.

DoD is charged with intercepting, countering, and defeating air threats to the United States. DoD and partner agencies position and operate aircraft in the United States and its territories for this mission, and DoD maintains specialized ground-based air defense assets in the National Capital Region. These assets must remain prepared for rapid interception of aircraft exhibiting anomalous behavior, even when the intent of the pilot is unknown due to constraints of time and communication. Early detection of potential threats through near real-time cooperation with the FAA and DHS, pre-incident planning, and operational response protocols are vital for assessing pilot intent and informing decision-making prior to application of non-lethal and, if necessary, lethal measures.

Capable and responsive maritime forces

DoD will improve maritime defense by developing complementary capabilities and enhancing interoperability with DHS.

DoD and DHS both have roles, responsibilities, capabilities, and authorities for conducting maritime operations. Navy assets are postured in coordination with the Coast Guard to counter potential maritime threats at a safe distance. DoD and DHS rely on well-exercised agreements for the expeditious transfer of Navy and Coast Guard assets to intercept emergent maritime threats and provide support to maritime homeland security. They will maintain an active routine of maritime interception exercises to ensure a high state of readiness and interoperability.

Objective 1.b: Prevent terrorist attacks on the homeland through support to law enforcement

As described earlier in this Strategy, the terrorist threat to the homeland is complex and multi-dimensional. Successfully preventing an attack requires the integration of authorities and capabilities among governmental, private sector, and international partners. DoD also has an inherent responsibility to keep its uniformed and civilian personnel safe, and protecting the force permeates every aspect of mission success. DoD personnel remain at high risk of harm from terrorists and other malicious actors due to their visibility and political value. An attack on DoD personnel could also directly impact the Department's ability to project power overseas, carry out vital homeland defense functions, or provide support to civil authorities.[8]

To maximize DoD anti-terrorism support to other Federal departments and agencies and to address concerns regarding threats to DoD personnel, the Department must preserve or expand its capabilities for supporting law enforcement and homeland security agencies in six defined areas in the period to 2020:

- Rapid and actionable intelligence on terrorist threats;

- Capabilities to counter IEDs;

- Capabilities to prevent terrorists' use of WMD in the homeland;

- Rapid acquisition, analysis and dissemination of threat information;

- Programs to counter insider threats; and

- Dual-effect military training.

Rapid and actionable intelligence on terrorist threats

DoD will maintain and enhance the Joint Intelligence Task Force for Combating Terrorism (JITF-CT) as its key node for sharing intelligence with interagency partners on terrorist threats. DoD will improve and refine intelligence and information-sharing relationships that have developed since 9/11 and as a result of the Fort Hood shootings.

DoD maintains a robust array of foreign intelligence capabilities, and sharing relevant counterterrorism-related information with the Federal Bureau of Investigations (FBI) and other key parties is vital to the prevention of potential terrorist threats to the homeland. JITF-CT will remain the focal point for DoD's outreach and sharing of intelligence and information with the FBI, the Office of the Director of National Intelligence (ODNI), and the National Counterterrorism Center (NCTC). Additionally, DoD will expand its participation within the various FBI Joint Terrorism Task Forces (JTTFs),[9] as well as other similar entities to maximize "top-down" and "bottom-up" sharing of key pieces of intelligence and information, consistent with applicable law and policy.

Capabilities to counter IEDs

DoD must maintain its hard-won expertise and capabilities in countering improvised explosive devices (IEDs) so that it is able to provide counter-IED (C-IED) support to Federal civilian agencies responsible for protecting against the IED threat to the homeland.

---

[8] DoD plays a key role in preventing terrorist attacks on the homeland by conducting military operations overseas, including ongoing operations in Afghanistan, as well as building partner capacity to defeat terrorists and support stability. These critical missions are highlighted in the 2010 *QDR* and 2012 *Defense Strategic Guidance*.

[9] DoD participation in JTTFs is programmed to grow to 120+ military personnel by the end of FY13.

DoD has developed unique and expansive C-IED capabilities in Iraq and Afghanistan. This includes the ability to identify threat networks that employ and/or facilitate IEDs; detect IEDs and IED components; prevent and neutralize IEDs; mitigate the effects of IED attacks; distribute IED-related data across the community of interest; and train C-IED forces. These capabilities have significant applicability to the civilian-led law enforcement C-IED mission in the homeland. DoD must preserve these capabilities, share lessons learned from combat missions, and support other Federal agencies, as authorized by law, to prevent, respond to, recover from, and mitigate IED attacks and their consequences. Additionally, as adversaries pursue new asymmetric tactics and techniques, DoD must harmonize its C-IED research and development efforts with those of the FBI and DHS and other relevant partners.

Capabilities to prevent terrorists' use of WMD in the homeland

Upon request of the Attorney General, DoD will provide rapid support to Federal law enforcement agencies for preventing a terrorist WMD attack in the homeland.

Consistent with statutory authority and under the PPD-8 Prevention Framework, DoD provides a wide range of enabling and support capabilities to Federal law enforcement agencies to prevent terrorist use of WMD in the homeland. DoD may provide certain logistical, intelligence and operational support upon request. The Department will continue to work closely with other Federal departments and agencies to develop plans (such as the Interagency Radiological/Nuclear Search Operations Plan) that address the provision of military-specific capabilities and inform expectations for DoD prevention assistance in the future.

Rapid acquisition, analysis, and dissemination of threat information

DoD will expand the use of law enforcement tools to improve threat awareness and suspicious activity reporting.

The USG has taken major steps to improve information sharing between the IC and the rest of the national security apparatus over the past decade. For example, the National Security Staff leads an interagency Information Sharing Environment through which DoD and other agencies regularly share terrorism-related information.

The *Fort Hood Follow-on Review* gives further impetus to intra-DoD and interagency information sharing activities. The FBI is a particularly valuable partner in support of DoD's responsibility to protect the force, and DoD will complete the deployment and expand the use of the FBI's eGuardian system and the Terrorist Screening Database to vet persons seeking access to Defense facilities and identify suspected terrorists. DoD will also develop a comprehensive counter-terrorism vetting policy and leverage applicable interagency identity intelligence systems to screen job applicants, foreign defense visitors, international military students, and contractors.

Programs to counter insider threats

DoD will develop, implement, and refine policies and programs to identify potential insider threats, along with response programs to minimize the effects of an attack if prevention fails.

The 2009 attack at Fort Hood and the *Fort Hood Follow-on Review* have led DoD to increase its focus on minimizing insider threats. DoD will endeavor to detect and act on early warning signs that an insider may pose a danger to DoD personnel or, more broadly, to national security.

Detection and prevention of insider threats require decisive, integrated planning, processes, and protocols. Key requirements in this area include:

- guidance that regularly familiarizes leaders with behavioral concerns that may indicate an insider threat;

- well-understood reporting procedures to document behavioral concerns and initiate investigations or threat assessments by multi-discipline experts in threat management and by terrorism analysts; and

- the ability to provide commanders with sufficient awareness of personnel whose behavior may adversely affect the safety of a unit.

DoD must also have plans and capabilities in place to provide effective emergency response should an insider attack take place. Regular training and awareness are vital to an effective response capability. DoD installations must have emergency management programs that include "Enhanced 911" emergency call location-finding and mass notification and warning systems for installation populations, thereby reducing the effects of insider threat violence and other accidents or incidents.

Dual-effect military training

DoD will expand efforts to identify opportunities to match the Services' military training requirements with Federal law enforcement agency support requirements where practicable.

DoD will deepen collaboration with Federal law enforcement agencies to maximize military training opportunities that concurrently and legally support Federal law enforcement and homeland security operational requirements.[10] Such "dual-effect" training can meet military training requirements and DoD's role in support of Federal law enforcement agencies in the performance of certain law enforcement missions. Where possible, the Department will consider law enforcement needs in the planning and execution of military training.

Mission 2: Provide Defense Support of Civil Authorities

DoD has a long history of providing support to civilian authorities when directed by the President, or in response to a formal request for assistance.[11] The Department has established policy and procedures for DSCA and has made significant investments to improve DoD's response to requests for support from civil authorities. DoD support will remain a vital element

---

[10] DoD personnel are generally restricted by the Posse Comitatus Act (10 U.S.C. § 375) and DoD policy from participating in civilian law enforcement activities within the United States. Such restrictions apply to dual-effect military training.

[11] Historical examples of DSCA include deployments in support of law enforcement along the southwestern U.S. border; support for pre-planned National Special Security Events (like summits and high-profile sports events); and response to imminent or no-notice events like wildfires, hurricanes, and earthquakes.

in a national approach to prevention, protection, mitigation, response, and recovery operations in the homeland.[12]

State and local authorities have extensive emergency management and "first responder" capabilities, but they may be overwhelmed in certain situations and request Federal assistance. Likewise, civilian agencies have significant capacity to execute FEMA-developed mission assignments for responding to a State's request for assistance, but they may also request DoD assistance based on the scale or scope of the incident and related response requirements.

Defense support is primarily drawn from the existing warfighting capabilities of the Armed Forces, and it can take the form of capabilities that are programmed and optimized for use in the homeland (such as CBRN consequence management response forces); capabilities that are deployable for DoD overseas missions but have relevance in the homeland (for example, technologies for countering IEDs); or capabilities and capacity resident in general purpose forces. Furthermore, military training may be planned and conducted in a manner that provides a dual effect, enhancing military readiness while having the additional effect of benefiting civil authorities (such as Customs and Border Protection).

Objective 2.a: Maintain defense preparedness for domestic CBRN incidents

Various national-level and DoD strategic guidance documents identify the threats posed to the United States by the proliferation of WMD. Since 2005, DoD has made significant capability investments as directed by the 2010 *QDR* and reinforced by the 2012 *Defense Strategic Guidance* to detect, protect against, and – should prevention fail – respond to multiple, simultaneous attacks or incidents involving CBRN materials in the homeland.

Detecting, preventing, mitigating and responding to CBRN incidents requires specially trained and equipped response forces which are postured for rapid deployment. DoD must preserve its CBRN response capabilities including specialized agent detection, identification, and dispersion modeling systems as well as casualty extraction and mass decontamination capabilities. DoD general purpose forces are also core components of the military CBRN incident response force and include medical, security, engineering, logistics and transportation capabilities. The Department will also maintain trained and equipped command-and-control capabilities to manage the specialized and general purpose forces that will likely be needed to support civilian agencies after a CBRN incident.

Postured and rapidly deployable CBRN response forces

DoD will maintain a CBRN response enterprise that balances Federal and State military responsibilities in order to reduce the response times to save lives and minimize human suffering. DoD will continue to improve CBRN force posturing and refine force sourcing processes to meet future national requirements for domestic CBRN incident response.

---

[12] In accordance with DoDD 3025.18, 31 U.S.C § 1535 (Economy Act), and 42 U.S.C. § 5121 et. seq. (Stafford Act), DoD approves requests for assistance using the following criteria: legality (compliance with laws); (2) lethality (potential use of lethal force by or against DoD personnel); (3) risk (safety of DoD personnel); (4) cost (including the source of funding and the effect on the DoD budget); (5) appropriateness (whether providing the requested support is in the interest of DoD); and, (6) readiness (impact on the DoD's ability to perform its primary mission).

Based on analysis in the 2010 *QDR*, DoD restructured its CBRN response forces to re-balance capabilities between the Reserve Component (the National Guard and the non-National Guard Reserves) and the Active Component. The Department's CBRN response approach reflects the shared roles and responsibilities of the States and Federal Government.[13] Its elements are designed to be modular and fully scalable to provide a simultaneous State and Federal military response to multiple CBRN incidents.

At the State level:

- Weapons of Mass Destruction-Civil Support Teams (WMD-CSTs) in 54 States and Territories provide *identification and assessment* of CBRN hazards and advise first responders and follow-on forces.

- CBRN Enhanced Response Force Packages (CERFPs) in 17 States provide regionally focused *life-saving capabilities* – for example, emergency medical treatment, search and rescue, and decontamination.

- Homeland Response Forces (HRFs) in 10 States – one per FEMA region – provide specialized and rapidly deployable *life-saving capabilities* and *command and control*.

At the Federal level:

- The Defense CBRN Response Force (DCRF) – a brigade-size element with two force packages composed of a mix of Active and Reserve personnel – provides extensive *life-saving, logistics, sustainment, and command and control* capabilities to respond to incidents which exceed State-level response capabilities.

- Two Command and Control CBRN Response Elements (C2CREs) provide *command and control* for large follow-on forces, both general-purpose and specialized. The C2CREs can assist the DCRF in response to a catastrophic incident or deploy independently, and they maintain some organic life-saving capabilities.

Objective 2.b: Develop plans and procedures to ensure Defense Support of Civil Authorities during complex catastrophes

DoD has historically supported civil authorities in a wide variety of domestic contingencies, often in response to natural disasters. However, the 21st century security environment, the concentration of population in major urban areas, and the interconnected nature of critical infrastructures have all combined to fundamentally alter the scope and scale of "worst case" incidents for which DoD might be called upon to provide civil support. This environment creates the potential for complex catastrophes, with effects that would qualitatively and quantitatively exceed those experienced to date. In such events, the demand for DSCA would be unprecedented. Meeting this demand would be especially challenging if a cyber attack or other disruption of the electrical power grid creates cascading failures of critical infrastructure, threatening lives and greatly complicating DoD response operations.

---

[13] Although the DoD CBRN response forces are optimized for domestic response, the Department should be prepared to deploy pre-identified force packages composed of these forces to support our global partners when directed by the President.

DoD must be prepared to help civilian authorities save and protect lives during a complex catastrophe. An effective response will require investments in preparedness (planning, organizing, equipping, and training), improving concepts of operations, and better linking of established Federal and State capabilities and systems. The following areas represent the Department's priorities for preparedness and response to catastrophic events:

- Leveraging immediate response authority;

- Geographically proximate force-sourcing; and

- Ready access to non-National Guard Reserve forces.

Immediate response authority

DoD will explore methods to leverage "immediate response" authority[14] to provide life-saving and logistical capabilities to a broader geographic area.

There are many large and medium-size DoD installations throughout the United States with significant resident or tenant capabilities that provide immediate life-saving and life-sustaining support to their on-base population. "Immediate response" authority allows responsible DoD officials to provide support, when requested by civilian agencies, to local communities and to State and Federal officials in extreme conditions. A key to success in meeting the urgent requirements of a catastrophic incident is *time*. DoD will therefore explore methods to most effectively leverage immediate response authority to employ capabilities to save lives, mitigate property damage, and prevent human suffering during catastrophic incidents.

Geographically proximate force-sourcing

DoD will explore new concepts of operations to leverage the relative proximity of Defense installations to a disaster area to provide life-saving capabilities to local, State, and Federal authorities.

A key consideration for catastrophic events is that response elements have the highest probability to save lives within 72-96 hours after an incident.[15] To address this time constraint, DoD will explore force-sourcing options that include a unit's proximity to the affected area – in addition to its readiness level for overseas missions, which is the traditional driver for mission assignments – as a core consideration for sourcing for disaster response efforts. Additionally, the Department will develop a decision matrix to give senior DoD leaders a mechanism for expedited Defense

---

[14] DoDD 3025.18, Defense Support of Civil Authorities (DSCA)

[15] Response times conform to Emergency Support Function 9, "Search and Rescue," and are generally accepted throughout the Federal government as the "golden window" for life-saving response.

support during a complex catastrophe, while identifying effects and risks resulting from those decisions.

<u>Ready access to non-National Guard Reserve forces</u>

DoD will develop rules and modalities to execute its authority for involuntary Reserve mobilization for response to emergencies in the United States, including natural disasters.

The Secretary of Defense now has the authority for involuntary mobilization of non-National Guard Reservists for domestic disaster response. The geographic dispersion of Reserve units and their life-saving medical, decontamination, engineering, and other capabilities mandate consideration of Reserve employment for any Total Force response. The Department will develop, refine, and implement policy that facilitates rapid approval for Reserve activation and employment.

__Figure 6: Hurricane Sandy and Defense Support of Civil Authorities (DSCA)__

DoD's activities during and after Hurricane Sandy in 2012 represented the largest domestic disaster response since Hurricane Katrina in 2005. DoD adopted an active posture in advance of the storm's landfall in anticipation of expected requests for assistance from civil authorities and based on direction from the President – consistent with the increasing expectations described in this Strategy. This posture allowed the President and civil authorities to rely on DoD to provide the majority of Federal support in the immediate aftermath of the storm.

The scope, scale and duration of Hurricane Sandy fell short of the threshold for a complex catastrophe. However, the cascading effects of the failures of critical infrastructure in the New York-New Jersey metropolitan area resembled those of a potential complex catastrophe: 8 million people out of power in severe cold; major transport disturbances due to inoperable ferries and flooded tunnels; severe disruptions of the East Coast fuel distribution system, including 2,500 inoperable gas stations; and regional commerce at a near standstill due to the closure of the Port of New York.

DoD's experience during Hurricane Sandy validated many of the core objectives, capability priorities, and approaches of this Strategy, including: development of plans and procedures to ensure DSCA during complex catastrophes; promoting Federal-State unity of effort; conducting integrated interagency planning; conducting integrated regional disaster response planning; and advancing the Department's mission assurance initiatives.

III. STRATEGIC APPROACHES

Consistent with the 2012 *Defense Strategic Guidance*, the Department will pursue innovative, cost-cutting, and effective solutions to evolving problem sets. When translated to the realms of Homeland Defense and Defense Support of Civil Authorities, these efforts, or *strategic approaches*, support the comprehensive end state of ensuring that the U.S. homeland remains secure from direct attack and the joint force can ably support domestic civil authorities. Unlike the core capabilities identified earlier, these strategic approaches embody efforts that are either modifications to current DoD business practices or involve the development of Federal interagency and/or DoD-specific policy mechanisms without significant resource implications.

Strategic Approach	Capabilities and Activities
Assure DoD's Ability to Conduct Critical Missions	• Integrated mission assurance approach as elaborated in the *Mission Assurance Strategy*
Promote Federal-State Unity of Effort	• Trained and certified dual status commanders • Shared situational awareness • Enhanced State and local first responder capabilities
Conduct Integrated Planning With Federal and State Authorities	• Integrated interagency planning and capability development • Integrated regional disaster response planning
Expand North American Cooperation to Strengthen Civil Support	• Habitual relationships with Canada and Mexico for disaster response

Figure 7: Strategic Approaches, Capabilities, and Activities

Assure DoD's Ability to Conduct Critical Missions

DoD requires operational continuity for its mission essential functions in an all-threat, all-hazard operating environment. Potential adversaries seek the ability to cripple vital force projection, warfighting, and sustainment capabilities by targeting the military and civilian infrastructure and supply chains that support these functions. Natural hazards and technological failures also can cause disruptions with significant cascading downstream effects to DoD operations. Technical, geopolitical, and budgetary changes require a new approach to mission assurance. As articulated in detail in the 2012 *Mission Assurance Strategy*, DoD's evolving *mission assurance* approach integrates and synchronizes multiple risk management efforts to manage risk across DoD mission essential functions.[16]

---

[16] Including, but not limited to, DoD Antiterrorism Program; Physical Security; Chemical, Biological, Radiological, and Nuclear Defense; Force Protection; Defense Critical Infrastructure Protection; Continuity of Operations; Installation Emergency Management; and Information Assurance.

Integrated mission assurance approach as elaborated in the *Mission Assurance Strategy*

DoD will pursue a mission assurance approach across the Department and with external partners to better identify risk and resiliency tradeoffs and to prioritize mitigation efforts.

DoD's mission assurance approach will rely on four pillars:

Prioritize missions, functions and supporting assets, and capabilities. DoD will refine its processes for prioritizing assets and capabilities critical to continuous performance of its mission essential functions, expanding beyond the traditional focus on physical assets to include information systems, supporting infrastructure, and supply chains. Mission critical assets – such as defense facilities, equipment, networks, information systems, and supporting infrastructure – must be identified and prioritized to differentiate their level of importance for ensuring continuity of mission performance. Risk assessment and mitigation efforts and resources from across risk management programs will be informed by these priorities.

Develop and implement a comprehensive and integrated risk management framework. DoD will develop and use common criteria for risk assessment and analysis. Risk assessments related to performance of mission essential functions require consistent and commonly accepted criteria for collecting, analyzing, and linking vulnerability and consequence information horizontally across components, installations, and programs and vertically from the tactical to strategic levels. Risk information must be managed in a manner that supports cross-component mission assurance-related decision-making.

Use risk-informed decision making to optimize mitigation solutions. DoD requires a mission assurance advocacy framework that brings together those responsible for executing mission essential functions and those responsible for the security and resilience of critical assets and systems. Decision-makers across DoD, from installation commanders to senior officials, must make integrated and risk-informed decisions regarding capabilities development, resource prioritization, and future investments at the installation, component, and headquarters level.

Partner to reduce risk. Finally, DoD will partner with other government organizations, foreign governments, and the private sector to share threat and vulnerability information and risk mitigation efforts. DoD's engagement with external organizations helps to reduce or eliminate risk and build resiliency to physical and human assets, as well as cyber systems and networks. A key focus for DoD will be the expansion of interagency and private sector partnerships to provide energy surety.

Promote Federal-State Unity of Effort

Unity of effort between the Federal Government and States must be one of DoD's guiding principles in the homeland, since unifying DoD's efforts with those of its external partners improves collaboration and shortens response times for meeting life-saving needs during emergencies. Unity of effort also means greater national preparedness at less overall cost, while preserving both Federal and State constitutional requirements and responsibilities. DoD and its Federal partners must continue to strengthen unity of effort with States to define common goals regarding capabilities, structures, and processes for responses to disaster and emergencies in the homeland. The Council of Governors – established by Executive Order in 2010 – will be an essential forum for enhanced, senior-level dialogue among Federal and State civilian and military officials for this purpose.

As the Department seeks a closer and more highly coordinated relationship between Federal and State military disaster response elements, DoD will prioritize three capabilities and activities to achieve unity of effort in the period covered by this Strategy:

- Trained and certified dual-status commanders;

- Shared situational awareness; and

- Enhanced State and local first responder capabilities.

Trained and certified dual-status commanders

DoD will regard dual-status commanders as the usual and customary command and control arrangement in cases where Federal military and State National Guard forces are employed simultaneously in support of civil authorities within the United States.

The President may authorize a National Guard officer of a State or a commissioned officer of the Regular Army or the Regular Air Force to serve as a dual-status commander, with the consent of the applicable State or Territorial Governor. The dual-status commander has authority over both State military forces (i.e., National Guard forces in a State active duty status or in a Title 32 status) and Federal military forces. This authority allows the commander to coordinate and de-conflict Federal and State operational assignments while respecting the State and Federal chains of command.

DoD will continue to refine processes for dual-status commanders and their associated command structures. By leveraging the use of such commanders, DoD will improve Federal-State communication, economy of force, and force employment for planned events and no-notice or imminent incidents. Historic examples of the employment of dual status commanders include national special security events such as the Democratic and Republican national conventions and responses to disasters like Hurricane Sandy and wildfires in the western United States.

Shared situational awareness

DoD will promote shared situational awareness through the establishment of an unclassified but secure common operational picture (COP) between Federal and State military forces to enable the sharing of operational data regarding State and Federal military units, including location and availability status. DoD will pursue a solution that relies on access to common and relevant databases and makes this data available to all military stakeholders for use during incident response.

DoD, the States, and FEMA require shared situational awareness (SSA) to enhance overall unity of effort and adaptive decision making during disasters and other crises. As a step towards this national and integrated civil-military, multi-level situational awareness, DoD will first pursue a COP between Federal military forces and State National Guard forces.

A COP must allow operational commanders and senior-level decision makers to anticipate requirements and maintain situational awareness of concurrent activities of State and Federal military forces. Since Federal and State military components have varying requirements for relevant information and level of detail, development of a COP solution need not specify systems, hardware, or software. Instead, it must be based on *common data* from authoritative military or civilian databases that flow to various systems in a common format.

<u>Enhanced State and local first responder capabilities</u>

DoD will continue to refine its approach to distributing excess military property and sharing technology to enhance the counter-terrorism and disaster response capabilities of State and local authorities.

The Domestic Preparedness Support Initiative (DPSI) leverages the significant DoD investments in military technologies to assist State and local authorities in building their capacity and improving their capabilities for prevention and response. DoD will provide this assistance (as transfers, loans, and sales of technology) by identifying, evaluating, and distributing DoD technologies that have the potential to enhance public safety, improve homeland security, and increase overall civilian resilience. DPSI will continue to represent cost savings for DoD, law enforcement agencies, and the American taxpayer.

Conduct Integrated Planning with Federal and State Authorities

Integrated planning means effectively and proactively shaping interagency and national expectations for what DoD can contribute to national preparedness efforts. This Strategy recognizes that deliberate, systematic planning against a range of scenarios is a core, enduring DoD competency. Further enhancing liaison relationships and deeper integration of DoD planning capabilities with those of other Federal agencies like DHS and the Department of Justice is mutually desirable and essential. Such integration is necessary to help prepare for a range of potential catastrophes and respond rapidly with lifesaving capabilities in the critical timeframe after a disaster strikes.

Through Presidential Policy Directive-8 (National Preparedness), the United States now has a series of national planning frameworks and is developing interagency operational plans that will support each preparedness mission area: prevention, protection, mitigation, response, and recovery. Together, the frameworks and interagency plans outline DoD's roles and responsibilities as a key contributor to national preparedness efforts. Enhanced and deepened defense liaison relationships – at various Federal agency headquarters, at the ten FEMA regional offices, and with State governments – will be core enablers of strengthened Federal, regional, and State-level planning, training, and exercises for defense support of civil authorities.

Additionally, the Homeland Response Forces (HRFs) in each of the ten FEMA regions will provide a regional planning capability focused on CBRN incidents. Ensuring the seamless flow of intelligence and actionable information among DoD and national security, intelligence, and law enforcement partners – particularly in the context of preventing future terrorist attacks against the United States – is another key integrated planning imperative. This Strategy provides direction for expanding and deepening information sharing initiatives that have evolved since 9/11 to strengthen indications and warnings, ensure coordinated planning before a crisis, and enable rapid, informed decision-making processes during an emergency.

DoD can strengthen the national planning enterprise through:

- Integrated interagency planning and capability development; and

- Integrated regional disaster response planning.

Integrated interagency planning and capability development

DoD will remain an essential partner in Federal interagency planning efforts by providing DoD-specific expertise and military capabilities to support an integrated approach to national preparedness. The Department will also maintain current capability development efforts with DHS to research, acquire, and deploy novel technologies that mutually support the defense and security of the homeland.

DoD's well-developed, systematic, and adaptable approach to planning is vital to strengthening the national mission areas elaborated in PPD-8, whose frameworks and interagency plans will form the basis for national preparedness across the Federal Government. DoD must ensure that planning for homeland defense and civil support adequately supports each mission area and facilitates the execution of DoD roles and responsibilities. The PPD-8 process helps ensure that DoD skills and capabilities are well integrated into the Federal Government's plans for full-spectrum support missions in response to a range of potential national threats and hazards.

DoD will work to nurture new collaborative research, development, experimentation, test and acquisition opportunities with DHS, while avoiding duplication of effort in these areas. Such collaboration can increase the effectiveness of national capabilities and potentially reduce other agencies' dependence on DoD assets. This collaboration may take the form of working groups or the exploration of joint requirements for homeland defense and homeland security.

Integrated, regional disaster response planning

DoD will use the planning capacity of Defense Coordinating Elements (DCEs) to expand planning cooperation at the regional level so that Departmental capabilities are considered in FEMA-led regional planning efforts. DoD will also build an integrated organizational architecture for its liaison and coordinating officers at various headquarters.

The ten FEMA regional offices are key nodes for integrating Federal plans with State and local plans, and DCEs within these regional offices are essential for operational and tactical unity of effort in an adaptive environment. This regional planning relationship bridges the gap between State-level planning conducted at a National Guard's Joint Force Headquarters (JFHQ)-State and DoD and DHS national-level planning. The JFHQs in each of the 54 States and Territories provide vital ties to State emergency officials and the National Guard Bureau. This enduring synergy positions the JFHQ as the key State-level organization for integrating the emergency plans of local DoD installations with State plans and FEMA regional plans.

DoD will deepen and facilitate rigorous Federal, regional, and State-level planning, training, and exercises through coordination and liaison arrangements that support civil authorities at all levels. These arrangements include DoD liaison officers at DHS and FEMA, Defense Coordinating Officers (DCOs), and Emergency Preparedness Liaison Officers from each Service in all States and Territories. This support architecture will require additional Departmental focus to systematically elaborate roles, responsibilities, and relationships of designated personnel so that they may more effectively develop disaster preparedness and response plans; improve State and Federal training and exercises; assess and catalogue civilian and military capabilities; and help identify capability gaps. Additionally, the Homeland Response Forces hosted by ten States provide further capacity for integrated, regional planning focused on CBRN incidents.

Expand North American Cooperation to Strengthen Civil Support

The United States faces threats, hazards and vulnerabilities in concert with its neighbors: natural disasters like hurricanes, floods, and earthquakes frequently transcend national borders. Additionally, the United States and its neighbors collectively face challenges associated with industrial accidents, environmental mishaps, violent extremists, transnational organized crime, and malicious cyber actors. From an interdependency perspective, the United States shares significant cross-border transportation, communication, and energy grid infrastructure with Canada and Mexico. Comprehensively reducing risk to the U.S. homeland therefore requires extending defense partnerships with our immediate North American neighbors – Canada and Mexico.

Extending these partnerships builds on a solid foundation of military cooperation. The United States and Canada maintain a bi-national military command – the North American Aerospace Defense Command, or NORAD – for aerospace defense and maritime warning. NORAD, USNORTHCOM, and the Canadian Joint Operations Command continue to build closer cooperation through the Canada-United States (CANUS) Combined Defense Plan and a CANUS Civil Assistance Plan. The United States and Mexico collaborate on cross-border security matters in various forums, including at the Joint Interagency Task Force-South. These mechanisms for cooperation represent valuable tools to secure our homeland and assist our neighbors in the event of a catastrophe or international threat.

Habitual relationships with Canada and Mexico for disaster response

DoD will seek novel ways to provide and receive support from North American neighbors in the event of a natural or manmade catastrophe.

Habits of cooperation and shared capabilities are essential in facilitating the integration of North American civil support assets in cases of U.S.-based catastrophic incidents or deployment of U.S. military forces when neighboring governments request humanitarian or disaster relief assistance from the United States. DoD will work with the Department of State to expand opportunities for mutual aid with Canada and Mexico and develop habitual support relationships with their defense establishments via planning, training, and exercising. These activities will strengthen mutual security at lower overall cost through shared approaches to national operational requirements.

IV. CONCLUSION

The United States continues to confront dynamic and focused adversaries. Our enemies seek new, innovative ways to attack our country where it is most vulnerable and to maximize the psychological, economic, and military impact of their attacks. At the same time, our Nation is also susceptible to natural and manmade catastrophes, some of which may be so severe that they require a truly national response to save lives, protect property, and restore the affected areas to normalcy. As we rebalance our forces abroad, the Department must consider the challenges it faces in protecting the homeland. Accordingly, this Strategy imparts the Department's vision for its role in the homeland from 2012 to 2020.

The Department relies on an active, layered defense – a global defense in-depth in all domains – to prevent attacks on the homeland by denying and defeating aggressors abroad, in the global commons, and in the approaches to the United States. As a part of this global defense, the Department conducts its enduring homeland defense and civil support missions; evaluates, prioritizes, and mitigates risks to its mission essential functions; provides accurate, timely, and effective support to Federal law enforcement efforts; and drives initiatives to improve unity of effort and integrated planning with the Department's Federal, State, local, Tribal and private sector partners.

The objectives, core capabilities, and strategic approaches outlined in this Strategy are intended to steer the Department towards wise investments in an era of fiscal constraint and to maximize taxpayer value – at a time when public expectations for the Federal Government's assistance are at an all-time high. Where possible, this Strategy emphasizes policy and planning approaches and seeks to develop novel, non-material solutions to problems rather than investing in new equipment and capabilities. In some high priority areas, however, the Department must and will continue to invest – particularly in the CBRN consequence management enterprise, counter-IED technologies, and the elements of our counter-terrorism information sharing and fusion architecture.

Since the 2005 *Strategy for Homeland Defense and Civil Support* broke ground on the Department's role in the homeland much has improved, and much has changed. This Strategy seeks to chart an effective and fiscally sustainable course for the Department over the mid- to long-term. Though the next decade will undoubtedly bring new challenges and threats, the Department will continue to honor its most solemn duty to defend the homeland – our people, our property, and our freedom.

www.ingramcontent.com/pod-product-compliance
Lightning Source LLC
Chambersburg PA
CBHW080755290526
45790CB00008B/3454